Elias Hill
101 So Bad, They're Good Teacher Jokes
Copyright 2017
Self-published, Tiny Camel Books

Tiny Camel Books
tinycamelbooks.com
tinycamelbooks@gmail.com

101

So Bad, They're Good

Teacher Jokes

By: Elias Hill

Illustrations By: Katherine Hogan

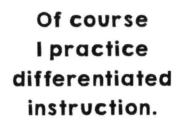

Waiting for the copier and being like,

"Will you be finished making your class set of dictionaries soon?"

The test is worth 100 points. You would need 135 points to earn a D for the quarter.

And how many points would I need to get a C?

And so a man, who is very unhappy with his life, wakes up to find he has been transformed into a large insect.

Is this fiction or nonfiction?

What do you call a teacher without a job?

Broke.

Oh wait, that's a regular teacher.

Who says teaching is stressful?

I'm 39 and I feel great!

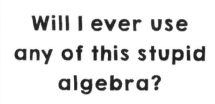

I got 99 problems...

and you're going to show your work on each and every one of them.

I don't think I deserved a "0" on this test.

I don't either, but it's the lowest score I could give you.

There is one person in our district who is all about *No Child Left Behind.*

The bus driver.

You copied from Julie's exam didn't you?

How do you know?

Julies's paper says "I don't know" and you wrote "Me, neither"!

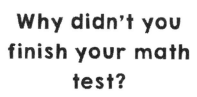

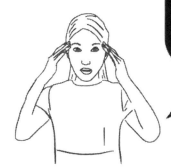

Let me guess, your dog ate your homework.

No, the cloud did.

What did the ghost teacher say to her class?

Look at the board and I'll go through it again.

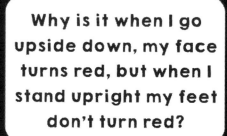

Why is it when I go upside down, my face turns red, but when I stand upright my feet don't turn red?

Because your feet aren't empty.

We'll only have half a day of school this morning.

We'll have the other half this afternoon.

Always follow your dreams.

Then you won't mind if I sleep in class?

Casey, I hope I didn't see you looking at Ella's paper.

I hope so too.

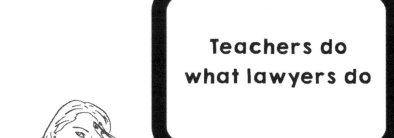

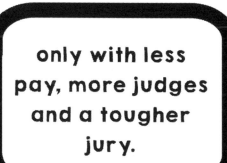

I was not feeling well the day I took this test.

I can believe that. Some of your answers made me a little sick, too.

Ethan, where is your homework?

I lost it fighting a kid who said you weren't the best teacher in the school.

Danielle, I wish you paid a little attention.

I'm paying as little as I can.

Here's a picture of us having fun at the last staff meeting.

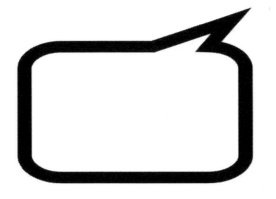

Yeah, I couldn't picture that either.

Setting a teacher's salary based on student performance

is like paying a zookeeper based on how well the monkeys are getting along.

When comforting a grammar teacher,

always say, "there, they're, their..."

I just had the worst class. First I got arteriosclerosis. Then psoriasis. And finally tonsillitis.

These spelling tests are getting out of control!

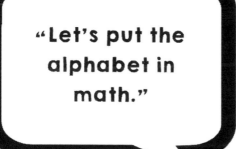

We named our copier "Bob Marley"

because it's always jammin'.

I told you to stand at the end of the line.

I tried, but there was someone already there!

This in-service training has just been fabulous!

Said no teacher ever.

Always start your sentence with "I am..."

I am the ninth letter of the alphabet.

Why are your eyes crossed?

I can't control my pupils.

I love all my students equally, except for the ones who are absent.

I love them the most.

Once I get this done and laminated I'll be set for years.

Oh look, new curriculum!

We'd be able to better educate our students if we taught through June.

Said no teacher ever.

Those who can, TEACH.

Those who can't,

pass laws about teaching.

I wrote all my lessons on the windows today.

Just so they were clear.

Teaching is easy. It's just like riding a bike.

Except the bike is on fire and you're on fire and everything is on fire because you're in hell.

I once told a
chemistry joke
to my class.

There was no
reaction.

Why, yes, I'd love to have a meeting,

about the meeting.

Tina, what's the longest sentence you can think of?

Life imprisonment.

> **What is the difference between a cat and a comma?**

> **One has claws at the end of its paws and the other is a pause at the end of a clause.**

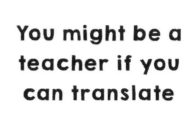

When I die, I hope it's during a teacher in-service.

The transition from life to death would be so subtle.

When I started teaching I wanted to change the world.

Now I'm thrilled if I remember to change the date on the board.

Why was the math teacher late?

He took the rhombus.

I don't always care about my grade.

But when I do it's at the end of the quarter and I haven't done any work but I'll ask for extra credit.

Please pay attention.

I can explain it to you, but I can't understand it for you.

But instead of me explaining it,

I'll turn it over to Mr. Nye.

The two most dreaded words in the English language,

indoor recess.

Of course we can schedule another parent conference

to discuss the same things I've been telling you about your child since day one.

Differentiate instruction, but standardize tests...

Interesting.

If you'd like a grade you shoulda put your name on it...

If you'd like a grade you shoulda put your name on it...whoa oh oh, oh oh oh..

If you can read this, thank a teacher.

Iff u kin reed dis, u prubly r ah teechr.

Well, one thing positive about your son,

with grades like these, he couldn't be cheating.

Are you going to "ask" me or "axe" me?

Because one of those involves murder.

The best thing about in-service days?

Going out to lunch.

Teachers waking up from a nap during the summer are like,

What happened? What year is it? Where are my students?

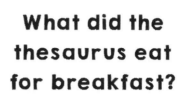

What did the thesaurus eat for breakfast?

A synonym roll.

I was arrested at the airport for carrying a protractor and a calculator.

Apparently those are weapons of math instruction.

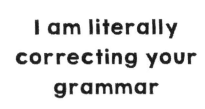

Why won't you turn in your essay?

Because I'm not a tattletale.

This math teacher gets mean,

median and mode.

They all call me the hot teacher

because my air vents never work.

All this time I thought PTA stood for

Parents To Avoid.

If you say
"I seen..."

then I'll assume
that sentence will
never be finished
with "the inside
of a book."

Printed in Poland
by Amazon Fulfillment
Poland Sp. z o.o., Wrocław

51634515R00060